Dulce et Decorum Est and Other Poems
by Wilfred Owens

With an Introduction by Siegfried Sassoon

Includes MLA Style Citations for Scholarly Secondary Sources, Peer-Reviewed Journal Articles and Critical Essays

DISCARD

Ingram 6/18 $8.10

Dulce et Decorum Est and Other Poems by Wilfred Owens

With an Introduction by Siegfried Sassoon

A Squid Ink Classic

[Squid Ink Classics Edition]

August 2016

Boston, MA

Dedicated to T. Messner

Introduction

In writing an Introduction such as this it is good to be brief. The poems printed in this book need no preliminary commendations from me or anyone else. The author has left us his own fragmentary but impressive Foreword; this, and his Poems, can speak for him, backed by the authority of his experience as an infantry soldier, and sustained by nobility and originality of style. All that was strongest in Wilfred Owen survives in his poems; any superficial impressions of his personality, any records of his conversation, behaviour, or appearance, would be irrelevant and unseemly. The curiosity which demands such morsels would be incapable of appreciating the richness of his work.

The discussion of his experiments in assonance and dissonance (of which 'Strange Meeting' is the finest example) may be left to the professional critics of verse, the majority of whom will be more preoccupied with such technical details than with the profound humanity of the self- revelation manifested in such magnificent lines as those at the end of his 'Apologia pro Poemate Meo', and in that other poem which he named 'Greater Love'.

The importance of his contribution to the literature of the War cannot be decided by those who, like myself, both admired him as a poet and valued him as a friend. His conclusions about War are so entirely in accordance with my own that I cannot attempt to judge his work with any critical detachment. I can only affirm that he was a man of absolute integrity of mind. He never wrote his poems (as so many war-poets did) to make the effect of a personal gesture. He pitied others; he did not pity himself. In the last year of his life he attained a clear vision of what he needed to say, and these poems survive him as his true and splendid testament.

Wilfred Owen was born at Oswestry on 18th March 1893. He was educated at the Birkenhead Institute, and matriculated at London University in 1910. In 1913 he obtained a private tutorship near Bordeaux, where he remained until 1915. During this period he became acquainted with the eminent French poet, Laurent Tailhade, to whom he showed his early verses, and from whom he received considerable encouragement. In 1915, in spite of delicate health, he joined the Artists' Rifles O.T.C., was gazetted to the Manchester Regiment, and served with their 2nd Battalion in France from December 1916 to June 1917, when he was invalided home. Fourteen months later he returned to the Western Front and served with the same Battalion, ultimately commanding a Company.

He was awarded the Military Cross for gallantry while taking part in some heavy fighting on 1st October. He was killed on 4th November 1918, while endeavouring to get his men across the Sambre Canal.

A month before his death he wrote to his mother: "My nerves are in perfect order. I came out again in order to help these boys; directly, by leading them as well as an officer can; indirectly, by watching their sufferings that I may speak of them as well as a pleader can." Let his own words be his epitaph:—

"Courage was mine, and I had mystery;

Wisdom was mine, and I had mastery."

Siegfried Sassoon.

Preface

This book is not about heroes. English Poetry is not yet fit to speak of them. Nor is it about deeds or lands, nor anything about glory, honour, dominion or power,

    except War.

  Above all, this book is not concerned with Poetry.

  The subject of it is War, and the pity of War.

  The Poetry is in the pity.

  Yet these elegies are not to this generation,

    This is in no sense consolatory.

  They may be to the next.

  All the poet can do to-day is to warn.

  That is why the true Poets must be truthful.

  If I thought the letter of this book would last,

I might have used proper names; but if the spirit of it survives

  Prussia,—my ambition and those names will be content; for they will

  have achieved themselves fresher fields than Flanders.

    Note.—This Preface was found, in an unfinished condition,

    among Wilfred Owen's papers.

CONTENTS

Introduction

POEMS

Preface

Dulce et Decorum est

Strange Meeting

Greater Love

Apologia pro Poemate Meo

The Show

Mental Cases

Parable of the Old Men and the Young

Arms and the Boy

Anthem for Doomed Youth

The Send-off

Insensibility

The Sentry

The Dead-Beat

Exposure

Spring Offensive

The Chances

S. I. W.

Futility

Smile, Smile, Smile

Conscious

A Terre

Wild with all Regrets

Disabled

Dulce et Decorum est

Bent double, like old beggars under sacks,

Knock-kneed, coughing like hags, we cursed through sludge,

Till on the haunting flares we turned our backs,

And towards our distant rest began to trudge.

Men marched asleep. Many had lost their boots,

But limped on, blood-shod. All went lame, all blind;

Drunk with fatigue; deaf even to the hoots

Of gas-shells dropping softly behind.

Gas! GAS! Quick, boys!—An ecstasy of fumbling

Fitting the clumsy helmets just in time,

But someone still was yelling out and stumbling

And flound'ring like a man in fire or lime.—

Dim through the misty panes and thick green light,

As under a green sea, I saw him drowning.

In all my dreams before my helpless sight

He plunges at me, guttering, choking, drowning.

If in some smothering dreams, you too could pace

Behind the wagon that we flung him in,

And watch the white eyes writhing in his face,

His hanging face, like a devil's sick of sin,

If you could hear, at every jolt, the blood

Come gargling from the froth-corrupted lungs

Bitter as the cud

Of vile, incurable sores on innocent tongues,—

My friend, you would not tell with such high zest

To children ardent for some desperate glory,

The old Lie: Dulce et decorum est

Pro patria mori.

Strange Meeting

It seemed that out of the battle I escaped

Down some profound dull tunnel, long since scooped

Through granites which Titanic wars had groined.

Yet also there encumbered sleepers groaned,

Too fast in thought or death to be bestirred.

Then, as I probed them, one sprang up, and stared

With piteous recognition in fixed eyes,

Lifting distressful hands as if to bless.

And by his smile, I knew that sullen hall;

With a thousand fears that vision's face was grained;

Yet no blood reached there from the upper ground,

And no guns thumped, or down the flues made moan.

"Strange, friend," I said, "Here is no cause to mourn."

"None," said the other, "Save the undone years,

The hopelessness. Whatever hope is yours,

Was my life also; I went hunting wild

After the wildest beauty in the world,

Which lies not calm in eyes, or braided hair,

But mocks the steady running of the hour,

And if it grieves, grieves richlier than here.

For by my glee might many men have laughed,

And of my weeping something has been left,

Which must die now. I mean the truth untold,

The pity of war, the pity war distilled.

Now men will go content with what we spoiled.

Or, discontent, boil bloody, and be spilled.

They will be swift with swiftness of the tigress,

None will break ranks, though nations trek from progress.

Courage was mine, and I had mystery;

Wisdom was mine, and I had mastery;

To miss the march of this retreating world

Into vain citadels that are not walled.

Then, when much blood had clogged their chariot-wheels

I would go up and wash them from sweet wells,

Even with truths that lie too deep for taint.

I would have poured my spirit without stint

But not through wounds; not on the cess of war.

Foreheads of men have bled where no wounds were.

I am the enemy you killed, my friend.

I knew you in this dark; for so you frowned

Yesterday through me as you jabbed and killed.

I parried; but my hands were loath and cold.

Let us sleep now . . ."

  (This poem was found among the author's papers.

  It ends on this strange note.)

Another Version

Earth's wheels run oiled with blood. Forget we that.

Let us lie down and dig ourselves in thought.

Beauty is yours and you have mastery,

Wisdom is mine, and I have mystery.

We two will stay behind and keep our troth.

Let us forego men's minds that are brute's natures,

Let us not sup the blood which some say nurtures,

Be we not swift with swiftness of the tigress.

Let us break ranks from those who trek from progress.

Miss we the march of this retreating world

Into old citadels that are not walled.

Let us lie out and hold the open truth.

Then when their blood hath clogged the chariot wheels

We will go up and wash them from deep wells.

What though we sink from men as pitchers falling

Many shall raise us up to be their filling

Even from wells we sunk too deep for war

And filled by brows that bled where no wounds were.

   Alternative line—

Even as One who bled where no wounds were.

Greater Love

   Red lips are not so red

      As the stained stones kissed by the English dead.

   Kindness of wooed and wooer

   Seems shame to their love pure.

   O Love, your eyes lose lure

      When I behold eyes blinded in my stead!

   Your slender attitude

      Trembles not exquisite like limbs knife-skewed,

   Rolling and rolling there

   Where God seems not to care;

Till the fierce Love they bear

    Cramps them in death's extreme decrepitude.

Your voice sings not so soft,—

    Though even as wind murmuring through raftered loft,—

Your dear voice is not dear,

Gentle, and evening clear,

As theirs whom none now hear

    Now earth has stopped their piteous mouths that coughed.

Heart, you were never hot,

    Nor large, nor full like hearts made great with shot;

And though your hand be pale,

Paler are all which trail

Your cross through flame and hail:

    Weep, you may weep, for you may touch them not.

Apologia pro Poemate Meo

   I, too, saw God through mud—

     The mud that cracked on cheeks when wretches smiled.

     War brought more glory to their eyes than blood,

     And gave their laughs more glee than shakes a child.

   Merry it was to laugh there—

     Where death becomes absurd and life absurder.

     For power was on us as we slashed bones bare

     Not to feel sickness or remorse of murder.

   I, too, have dropped off fear—

     Behind the barrage, dead as my platoon,

     And sailed my spirit surging, light and clear

     Past the entanglement where hopes lay strewn;

   And witnessed exultation—

     Faces that used to curse me, scowl for scowl,

     Shine and lift up with passion of oblation,

     Seraphic for an hour; though they were foul.

I have made fellowships—

    Untold of happy lovers in old song.

    For love is not the binding of fair lips

    With the soft silk of eyes that look and long,

By Joy, whose ribbon slips,—

    But wound with war's hard wire whose stakes are strong;

    Bound with the bandage of the arm that drips;

    Knit in the welding of the rifle-thong.

I have perceived much beauty

    In the hoarse oaths that kept our courage straight;

    Heard music in the silentness of duty;

    Found peace where shell-storms spouted reddest spate.

Nevertheless, except you share

    With them in hell the sorrowful dark of hell,

    Whose world is but the trembling of a flare,

    And heaven but as the highway for a shell,

You shall not hear their mirth:
> You shall not come to think them well content
> By any jest of mine. These men are worth
> Your tears: You are not worth their merriment.

November 1917.

The Show
> My soul looked down from a vague height with Death,
> As unremembering how I rose or why,
> And saw a sad land, weak with sweats of dearth,
> Gray, cratered like the moon with hollow woe,
> And fitted with great pocks and scabs of plaques.
>
> Across its beard, that horror of harsh wire,
> There moved thin caterpillars, slowly uncoiled.
> It seemed they pushed themselves to be as plugs
> Of ditches, where they writhed and shrivelled, killed.
>
> By them had slimy paths been trailed and scraped

Round myriad warts that might be little hills.

From gloom's last dregs these long-strung creatures crept,
And vanished out of dawn down hidden holes.

(And smell came up from those foul openings
As out of mouths, or deep wounds deepening.)

On dithering feet upgathered, more and more,
Brown strings towards strings of gray, with bristling spines,
All migrants from green fields, intent on mire.

Those that were gray, of more abundant spawns,
Ramped on the rest and ate them and were eaten.

I saw their bitten backs curve, loop, and straighten,
I watched those agonies curl, lift, and flatten.

Whereat, in terror what that sight might mean,
I reeled and shivered earthward like a feather.

And Death fell with me, like a deepening moan.

And He, picking a manner of worm, which half had hid

Its bruises in the earth, but crawled no further,

Showed me its feet, the feet of many men,

And the fresh-severed head of it, my head.

Mental Cases

Who are these? Why sit they here in twilight?

Wherefore rock they, purgatorial shadows,

Drooping tongues from jaws that slob their relish,

Baring teeth that leer like skulls' tongues wicked?

Stroke on stroke of pain,—but what slow panic,

Gouged these chasms round their fretted sockets?

Ever from their hair and through their hand palms

Misery swelters. Surely we have perished

Sleeping, and walk hell; but who these hellish?

—These are men whose minds the Dead have ravished.

Memory fingers in their hair of murders,

Multitudinous murders they once witnessed.
Wading sloughs of flesh these helpless wander,
Treading blood from lungs that had loved laughter.
Always they must see these things and hear them,
Batter of guns and shatter of flying muscles,
Carnage incomparable and human squander
Rucked too thick for these men's extrication.

Therefore still their eyeballs shrink tormented
Back into their brains, because on their sense
Sunlight seems a bloodsmear; night comes blood-black;
Dawn breaks open like a wound that bleeds afresh
—Thus their heads wear this hilarious, hideous,
Awful falseness of set-smiling corpses.
—Thus their hands are plucking at each other;
Picking at the rope-knouts of their scourging;
Snatching after us who smote them, brother,
Pawing us who dealt them war and madness.

Parable of the Old Men and the Young

So Abram rose, and clave the wood, and went,

And took the fire with him, and a knife.

And as they sojourned both of them together,

Isaac the first-born spake and said, My Father,

Behold the preparations, fire and iron,

But where the lamb for this burnt-offering?

Then Abram bound the youth with belts and straps,

And builded parapets and trenches there,

And stretch\ed forth the knife to slay his son.

When lo! an angel called him out of heaven,

Saying, Lay not thy hand upon the lad,

Neither do anything to him. Behold,

A ram caught in a thicket by its horns;

Offer the Ram of Pride instead of him.

But the old man would not so, but slew his son. . . .

Arms and the Boy

    Let the boy try along this bayonet-blade

    How cold steel is, and keen with hunger of blood;

    Blue with all malice, like a madman's flash;

And thinly drawn with famishing for flesh.

Lend him to stroke these blind, blunt bullet-heads
Which long to muzzle in the hearts of lads.
Or give him cartridges of fine zinc teeth,
Sharp with the sharpness of grief and death.

For his teeth seem for laughing round an apple.
There lurk no claws behind his fingers supple;
And God will grow no talons at his heels,
Nor antlers through the thickness of his curls.

Anthem for Doomed Youth
> What passing-bells for these who die as cattle?
>> Only the monstrous anger of the guns.
>> Only the stuttering rifles' rapid rattle
> Can patter out their hasty orisons.
> No mockeries for them; no prayers nor bells,
> Nor any voice of mourning save the choirs,—
> The shrill, demented choirs of wailing shells;

And bugles calling for them from sad shires.

What candles may be held to speed them all?
   Not in the hands of boys, but in their eyes
Shall shine the holy glimmers of goodbyes.
   The pallor of girls' brows shall be their pall;
Their flowers the tenderness of patient minds,
And each slow dusk a drawing-down of blinds.

The Send-off
   Down the close, darkening lanes they sang their way
   To the siding-shed,
   And lined the train with faces grimly gay.

   Their breasts were stuck all white with wreath and spray
   As men's are, dead.

   Dull porters watched them, and a casual tramp
   Stood staring hard,

Sorry to miss them from the upland camp.
Then, unmoved, signals nodded, and a lamp
Winked to the guard.

So secretly, like wrongs hushed-up, they went.
They were not ours:
We never heard to which front these were sent.

Nor there if they yet mock what women meant
Who gave them flowers.

Shall they return to beatings of great bells
In wild trainloads?
A few, a few, too few for drums and yells,
May creep back, silent, to still village wells
Up half-known roads.

Insensibility
    I

Happy are men who yet before they are killed

Can let their veins run cold.

Whom no compassion fleers

Or makes their feet

Sore on the alleys cobbled with their brothers.

The front line withers,

But they are troops who fade, not flowers

For poets' tearful fooling:

Men, gaps for filling

Losses who might have fought

Longer; but no one bothers.

 II

And some cease feeling

Even themselves or for themselves.

Dullness best solves

The tease and doubt of shelling,

And Chance's strange arithmetic

Comes simpler than the reckoning of their shilling.

They keep no check on Armies' decimation.

 III

Happy are these who lose imagination:

They have enough to carry with ammunition.

Their spirit drags no pack.

Their old wounds save with cold can not more ache.

Having seen all things red,

Their eyes are rid

Of the hurt of the colour of blood for ever.

And terror's first constriction over,

Their hearts remain small drawn.

Their senses in some scorching cautery of battle

Now long since ironed,

Can laugh among the dying, unconcerned.

   IV

Happy the soldier home, with not a notion

How somewhere, every dawn, some men attack,

And many sighs are drained.

Happy the lad whose mind was never trained:

His days are worth forgetting more than not.

He sings along the march

Which we march taciturn, because of dusk,

The long, forlorn, relentless trend

From larger day to huger night.

    V

We wise, who with a thought besmirch

Blood over all our soul,

How should we see our task

But through his blunt and lashless eyes?

Alive, he is not vital overmuch;

Dying, not mortal overmuch;

Nor sad, nor proud,

Nor curious at all.

He cannot tell

Old men's placidity from his.

    VI

But cursed are dullards whom no cannon stuns,

That they should be as stones.

Wretched are they, and mean

With paucity that never was simplicity.

By choice they made themselves immune

To pity and whatever mourns in man

Before the last sea and the hapless stars;

Whatever mourns when many leave these shores;

Whatever shares

The eternal reciprocity of tears.

The Sentry

    We'd found an old Boche dug-out, and he knew,

    And gave us hell, for shell on frantic shell

    Hammered on top, but never quite burst through.

    Rain, guttering down in waterfalls of slime

    Kept slush waist high, that rising hour by hour,

    Choked up the steps too thick with clay to climb.

    What murk of air remained stank old, and sour

    With fumes of whizz-bangs, and the smell of men

    Who'd lived there years, and left their curse in the den,

    If not their corpses. . . .

                  There we herded from the blast

Of whizz-bangs, but one found our door at last.

Buffeting eyes and breath, snuffing the candles.

And thud! flump! thud! down the steep steps came thumping

And splashing in the flood, deluging muck—

The sentry's body; then his rifle, handles

Of old Boche bombs, and mud in ruck on ruck.

We dredged him up, for killed, until he whined

"O sir, my eyes—I'm blind—I'm blind, I'm blind!"

Coaxing, I held a flame against his lids

And said if he could see the least blurred light

He was not blind; in time he'd get all right.

"I can't," he sobbed. Eyeballs, huge-bulged like squids

Watch my dreams still; but I forgot him there

In posting next for duty, and sending a scout

To beg a stretcher somewhere, and floundering about

To other posts under the shrieking air.

Those other wretches, how they bled and spewed,

And one who would have drowned himself for good,—

I try not to remember these things now.

Let dread hark back for one word only: how

Half-listening to that sentry's moans and jumps,

And the wild chattering of his broken teeth,

Renewed most horribly whenever crumps

Pummelled the roof and slogged the air beneath—

Through the dense din, I say, we heard him shout

"I see your lights!" But ours had long died out.

The Dead-Beat

    He dropped,—more sullenly than wearily,

    Lay stupid like a cod, heavy like meat,

    And none of us could kick him to his feet;

    Just blinked at my revolver, blearily;

    —Didn't appear to know a war was on,

    Or see the blasted trench at which he stared.

    "I'll do 'em in," he whined, "If this hand's spared,

    I'll murder them, I will."

                A low voice said,

"It's Blighty, p'raps, he sees; his pluck's all gone,

Dreaming of all the valiant, that AREN'T dead:

Bold uncles, smiling ministerially;

Maybe his brave young wife, getting her fun

In some new home, improved materially.

It's not these stiffs have crazed him; nor the Hun."

We sent him down at last, out of the way.

Unwounded;—stout lad, too, before that strafe.

Malingering? Stretcher-bearers winked, "Not half!"

Next day I heard the Doc.'s well-whiskied laugh:

"That scum you sent last night soon died. Hooray!"

Exposure
    I

    Our brains ache, in the merciless iced east winds that knife us . . .

    Wearied we keep awake because the night is silent . . .

Low drooping flares confuse our memory of the salient . . .

Worried by silence, sentries whisper, curious, nervous,
>> But nothing happens.

Watching, we hear the mad gusts tugging on the wire.
Like twitching agonies of men among its brambles.
Northward incessantly, the flickering gunnery rumbles,
Far off, like a dull rumour of some other war.
>> What are we doing here?

The poignant misery of dawn begins to grow . . .
We only know war lasts, rain soaks, and clouds sag stormy.
Dawn massing in the east her melancholy army
Attacks once more in ranks on shivering ranks of gray,
>> But nothing happens.

Sudden successive flights of bullets streak the silence.
Less deadly than the air that shudders black with snow,
With sidelong flowing flakes that flock, pause and renew,

 We watch them wandering up and down the wind's nonchalance,

  But nothing happens.

  II

 Pale flakes with lingering stealth come feeling for our faces—

 We cringe in holes, back on forgotten dreams, and stare, snow-dazed,

 Deep into grassier ditches. So we drowse, sun-dozed,

 Littered with blossoms trickling where the blackbird fusses.

  Is it that we are dying?

 Slowly our ghosts drag home: glimpsing the sunk fires glozed

 With crusted dark-red jewels; crickets jingle there;

 For hours the innocent mice rejoice: the house is theirs;

 Shutters and doors all closed: on us the doors are closed—

  We turn back to our dying.

 Since we believe not otherwise can kind fires burn;

 Nor ever suns smile true on child, or field, or fruit.

 For God's invincible spring our love is made afraid;

 Therefore, not loath, we lie out here; therefore were born,

  For love of God seems dying.

 To-night, His frost will fasten on this mud and us,

 Shrivelling many hands and puckering foreheads crisp.

 The burying-party, picks and shovels in their shaking grasp,

  Pause over half-known faces. All their eyes are ice,

   But nothing happens.

Spring Offensive

 Halted against the shade of a last hill,

 They fed, and, lying easy, were at ease

 And, finding comfortable chests and knees

 Carelessly slept. But many there stood still

 To face the stark, blank sky beyond the ridge,

 Knowing their feet had come to the end of the world.

Marvelling they stood, and watched the long grass swirled

By the May breeze, murmurous with wasp and midge,

For though the summer oozed into their veins

Like the injected drug for their bones' pains,

Sharp on their souls hung the imminent line of grass,

Fearfully flashed the sky's mysterious glass.

Hour after hour they ponder the warm field—

And the far valley behind, where the buttercups

Had blessed with gold their slow boots coming up,

Where even the little brambles would not yield,

But clutched and clung to them like sorrowing hands;

They breathe like trees unstirred.

Till like a cold gust thrilled the little word

At which each body and its soul begird

And tighten them for battle. No alarms

Of bugles, no high flags, no clamorous haste—

Only a lift and flare of eyes that faced

The sun, like a friend with whom their love is done.

O larger shone that smile against the sun,—

Mightier than his whose bounty these have spurned.

So, soon they topped the hill, and raced together

Over an open stretch of herb and heather

Exposed. And instantly the whole sky burned

With fury against them; and soft sudden cups

Opened in thousands for their blood; and the green slopes

Chasmed and steepened sheer to infinite space.

Of them who running on that last high place

Leapt to swift unseen bullets, or went up

On the hot blast and fury of hell's upsurge,

Or plunged and fell away past this world's verge,

Some say God caught them even before they fell.

But what say such as from existence' brink

Ventured but drave too swift to sink.

The few who rushed in the body to enter hell,

And there out-fiending all its fiends and flames

With superhuman inhumanities,

Long-famous glories, immemorial shames—

And crawling slowly back, have by degrees

Regained cool peaceful air in wonder—

Why speak they not of comrades that went under?

The Chances

I mind as 'ow the night afore that show

Us five got talking,—we was in the know,

"Over the top to-morrer; boys, we're for it,

First wave we are, first ruddy wave; that's tore it."

"Ah well," says Jimmy,—an' 'e's seen some scrappin'—

"There ain't more nor five things as can 'appen;

Ye get knocked out; else wounded—bad or cushy;

Scuppered; or nowt except yer feeling mushy."

One of us got the knock-out, blown to chops.

T'other was hurt, like, losin' both 'is props.

An' one, to use the word of 'ypocrites,

'Ad the misfortoon to be took by Fritz.

Now me, I wasn't scratched, praise God Almighty

(Though next time please I'll thank 'im for a blighty),

But poor young Jim, 'e's livin' an' 'e's not;

'E reckoned 'e'd five chances, an' 'e's 'ad;

'E's wounded, killed, and pris'ner, all the lot—

The ruddy lot all rolled in one. Jim's mad.

S. I. W.

    "I will to the King,

And offer him consolation in his trouble,

For that man there has set his teeth to die,

And being one that hates obedience,

Discipline, and orderliness of life,

I cannot mourn him."

              W. B. Yeats.

Patting goodbye, doubtless they told the lad

He'd always show the Hun a brave man's face;

Father would sooner him dead than in disgrace,—

Was proud to see him going, aye, and glad.

Perhaps his Mother whimpered how she'd fret

Until he got a nice, safe wound to nurse.

Sisters would wish girls too could shoot, charge, curse,

. . .

Brothers—would send his favourite cigarette,

Each week, month after month, they wrote the same,

Thinking him sheltered in some Y.M. Hut,

Where once an hour a bullet missed its aim

And misses teased the hunger of his brain.

His eyes grew old with wincing, and his hand

Reckless with ague. Courage leaked, as sand

From the best sandbags after years of rain.

But never leave, wound, fever, trench-foot, shock,

Untrapped the wretch. And death seemed still withheld

For torture of lying machinally shelled,

At the pleasure of this world's Powers who'd run amok.

He'd seen men shoot their hands, on night patrol,

Their people never knew. Yet they were vile.

"Death sooner than dishonour, that's the style!"

So Father said.

    One dawn, our wire patrol

Carried him. This time, Death had not missed.

We could do nothing, but wipe his bleeding cough.

Could it be accident?—Rifles go off . . .

Not sniped? No. (Later they found the English ball.)

It was the reasoned crisis of his soul.

Against the fires that would not burn him whole

But kept him for death's perjury and scoff

And life's half-promising, and both their riling.

With him they buried the muzzle his teeth had kissed,

And truthfully wrote the Mother "Tim died smiling."

Futility

    Move him into the sun—

    Gently its touch awoke him once,

    At home, whispering of fields unsown.

    Always it woke him, even in France,

Until this morning and this snow.
If anything might rouse him now
The kind old sun will know.

Think how it wakes the seeds—
Woke, once, the clays of a cold star.
Are limbs so dear-achieved, are sides
Full-nerved,—still warm,—too hard to stir?
Was it for this the clay grew tall?
—O what made fatuous sunbeams toil
To break earth's sleep at all?

Smile, Smile, Smile

    Head to limp head, the sunk-eyed wounded scanned
    Yesterday's Mail; the casualties (typed small)
    And (large) Vast Booty from our Latest Haul.
    Also, they read of Cheap Homes, not yet planned;
    For, said the paper, "When this war is done
    The men's first instinct will be making homes.
    Meanwhile their foremost need is aerodromes,

It being certain war has just begun.

Peace would do wrong to our undying dead,—

The sons we offered might regret they died

If we got nothing lasting in their stead.

We must be solidly indemnified.

Though all be worthy Victory which all bought,

We rulers sitting in this ancient spot

Would wrong our very selves if we forgot

The greatest glory will be theirs who fought,

Who kept this nation in integrity."

Nation?—The half-limbed readers did not chafe

But smiled at one another curiously

Like secret men who know their secret safe.

This is the thing they know and never speak,

That England one by one had fled to France

(Not many elsewhere now save under France).

Pictures of these broad smiles appear each week,

And people in whose voice real feeling rings

Say: How they smile! They're happy now, poor things.

23rd September 1918.

Conscious

    His fingers wake, and flutter up the bed.
    His eyes come open with a pull of will,
    Helped by the yellow may-flowers by his head.
    A blind-cord drawls across the window-sill . . .
    How smooth the floor of the ward is! what a rug!
    And who's that talking, somewhere out of sight?
    Why are they laughing? What's inside that jug?
    "Nurse! Doctor!" "Yes; all right, all right."

    But sudden dusk bewilders all the air—
    There seems no time to want a drink of water.
    Nurse looks so far away. And everywhere
    Music and roses burnt through crimson slaughter.
    Cold; cold; he's cold; and yet so hot:
    And there's no light to see the voices by—
    No time to dream, and ask—he knows not what.

A Terre

    (Being the philosophy of many Soldiers.)

Sit on the bed; I'm blind, and three parts shell,

Be careful; can't shake hands now; never shall.

Both arms have mutinied against me—brutes.

My fingers fidget like ten idle brats.

I tried to peg out soldierly—no use!

One dies of war like any old disease.

This bandage feels like pennies on my eyes.

I have my medals?—Discs to make eyes close.

My glorious ribbons?—Ripped from my own back

In scarlet shreds. (That's for your poetry book.)

A short life and a merry one, my brick!

We used to say we'd hate to live dead old,—

Yet now . . . I'd willingly be puffy, bald,

And patriotic. Buffers catch from boys

At least the jokes hurled at them. I suppose

Little I'd ever teach a son, but hitting,

Shooting, war, hunting, all the arts of hurting.

Well, that's what I learnt,—that, and making money.

Your fifty years ahead seem none too many?

Tell me how long I've got? God! For one year

To help myself to nothing more than air!

One Spring! Is one too good to spare, too long?

Spring wind would work its own way to my lung,

And grow me legs as quick as lilac-shoots.

My servant's lamed, but listen how he shouts!

When I'm lugged out, he'll still be good for that.

Here in this mummy-case, you know, I've thought

How well I might have swept his floors for ever,

I'd ask no night off when the bustle's over,

Enjoying so the dirt. Who's prejudiced

Against a grimed hand when his own's quite dust,

Less live than specks that in the sun-shafts turn,

Less warm than dust that mixes with arms' tan?

I'd love to be a sweep, now, black as Town,

Yes, or a muckman. Must I be his load?

O Life, Life, let me breathe,—a dug-out rat!

Not worse than ours the existences rats lead—

Nosing along at night down some safe vat,

They find a shell-proof home before they rot.

Dead men may envy living mites in cheese,

Or good germs even. Microbes have their joys,

And subdivide, and never come to death,

Certainly flowers have the easiest time on earth.

"I shall be one with nature, herb, and stone."

Shelley would tell me. Shelley would be stunned;

The dullest Tommy hugs that fancy now.

"Pushing up daisies," is their creed, you know.

To grain, then, go my fat, to buds my sap,

For all the usefulness there is in soap.

D'you think the Boche will ever stew man-soup?

Some day, no doubt, if . . .

                Friend, be very sure

I shall be better off with plants that share

More peaceably the meadow and the shower.

Soft rains will touch me,—as they could touch once,

And nothing but the sun shall make me ware.

Your guns may crash around me. I'll not hear;

Or, if I wince, I shall not know I wince.

Don't take my soul's poor comfort for your jest.
Soldiers may grow a soul when turned to fronds,
But here the thing's best left at home with friends.

My soul's a little grief, grappling your chest,
To climb your throat on sobs; easily chased
On other sighs and wiped by fresher winds.

Carry my crying spirit till it's weaned
To do without what blood remained these wounds.

Wild with all Regrets
    (Another version of "A Terre".)

    To Siegfried Sassoon
My arms have mutinied against me—brutes!
My fingers fidget like ten idle brats,
My back's been stiff for hours, damned hours.
Death never gives his squad a Stand-at-ease.
I can't read. There: it's no use. Take your book.

A short life and a merry one, my buck!

We said we'd hate to grow dead old. But now,

Not to live old seems awful: not to renew

My boyhood with my boys, and teach 'em hitting,

Shooting and hunting,—all the arts of hurting!

—Well, that's what I learnt. That, and making money.

Your fifty years in store seem none too many;

But I've five minutes. God! For just two years

To help myself to this good air of yours!

One Spring! Is one too hard to spare? Too long?

Spring air would find its own way to my lung,

And grow me legs as quick as lilac-shoots.

Yes, there's the orderly. He'll change the sheets

When I'm lugged out, oh, couldn't I do that?

Here in this coffin of a bed, I've thought

I'd like to kneel and sweep his floors for ever,—

And ask no nights off when the bustle's over,

For I'd enjoy the dirt; who's prejudiced

Against a grimed hand when his own's quite dust,—

Less live than specks that in the sun-shafts turn?

Dear dust,—in rooms, on roads, on faces' tan!

I'd love to be a sweep's boy, black as Town;

Yes, or a muckman. Must I be his load?

A flea would do. If one chap wasn't bloody,

Or went stone-cold, I'd find another body.

Which I shan't manage now. Unless it's yours.

I shall stay in you, friend, for some few hours.

You'll feel my heavy spirit chill your chest,

And climb your throat on sobs, until it's chased

On sighs, and wiped from off your lips by wind.

I think on your rich breathing, brother, I'll be weaned

To do without what blood remained me from my wound.

5th December 1917.

Disabled

He sat in a wheeled chair, waiting for dark,

And shivered in his ghastly suit of grey,

Legless, sewn short at elbow. Through the park
Voices of boys rang saddening like a hymn,
Voices of play and pleasure after day,
Till gathering sleep had mothered them from him.

About this time Town used to swing so gay
When glow-lamps budded in the light-blue trees
And girls glanced lovelier as the air grew dim,
—In the old times, before he threw away his knees.
Now he will never feel again how slim
Girls' waists are, or how warm their subtle hands,
All of them touch him like some queer disease.

There was an artist silly for his face,
For it was younger than his youth, last year.
Now he is old; his back will never brace;
He's lost his colour very far from here,
Poured it down shell-holes till the veins ran dry,
And half his lifetime lapsed in the hot race,
And leap of purple spurted from his thigh.
One time he liked a bloodsmear down his leg,

After the matches carried shoulder-high.

It was after football, when he'd drunk a peg,

He thought he'd better join. He wonders why . . .

Someone had said he'd look a god in kilts.

That's why; and maybe, too, to please his Meg,

Aye, that was it, to please the giddy jilts,

He asked to join. He didn't have to beg;

Smiling they wrote his lie; aged nineteen years.

Germans he scarcely thought of; and no fears

Of Fear came yet. He thought of jewelled hilts

For daggers in plaid socks; of smart salutes;

And care of arms; and leave; and pay arrears;

Esprit de corps; and hints for young recruits.

And soon, he was drafted out with drums and cheers.

Some cheered him home, but not as crowds cheer Goal.

Only a solemn man who brought him fruits

Thanked him; and then inquired about his soul.

Now, he will spend a few sick years in Institutes,

And do what things the rules consider wise,

And take whatever pity they may dole.

To-night he noticed how the women's eyes

Passed from him to the strong men that were whole.

How cold and late it is! Why don't they come

And put him into bed? Why don't they come?

The End

After the blast of lightning from the east,

The flourish of loud clouds, the Chariot throne,

After the drums of time have rolled and ceased

And from the bronze west long retreat is blown,

Shall Life renew these bodies? Of a truth

All death will he annul, all tears assuage?

Or fill these void veins full again with youth

And wash with an immortal water age?

When I do ask white Age, he saith not so,—

"My head hangs weighed with snow."

And when I hearken to the Earth she saith

My fiery heart sinks aching. It is death.

Mine ancient scars shall not be glorified

Nor my titanic tears the seas be dried."

MLA Style Citations for Scholarly Secondary Sources, Peer-Reviewed Journal Articles and Critical Essays

Banerjee, A. "Wilfred Owen-A Reassessment." The Literary Half-Yearly 18.2 (1977): 85-100. Rpt. in Poetry Criticism. Ed. Carol T. Gaffke. Vol. 19. Detroit: Gale, 1997. Literature Resource Center. Web.

Brophy, James D. "The War Poetry of Wilfred Owen and Osbert Sitwell: An Instructive Contrast." Modern Language Studies 1.2 (1971): 22-29. Web.

Burness, Edwina. "Service's 'Bonehead Bill' and Owen's 'Strange Meeting.'." Explicator 43.3 (Spring 1985): 24-26. Rpt. in Poetry Criticism. Ed. Michelle Lee. Vol. 70. Detroit: Gale, 2006. Literature Resource Center. Web.

Campbell, James. "Combat Gnosticism: The Ideology of First World War Poetry Criticism." New Literary History 30.1 (1999): 203-15. Web.

Cole, Sarah. "Enchantment, Disenchantment, War, Literature." PMLA 124.5 (2009): 1632-647. Web.

Cyr, Marc D. "The conscientious killer: Wilfred Owen's 'Strange Meeting'." Texas Studies in Literature and Language 58.1 (2016): 108+. Literature Resource Center. Web.

Drew, Chris, and Yost David. "Composing Creativity: Further Crossing Composition/Creative Writing Boundaries." The Journal of the Midwest Modern Language Association 42.1 (2009): 25-42. Web.

Gose, Elliott B. "Digging In: An Interpretation of Wilfred Owen's "Strange Meeting""College English 22.6 (1961): 417-19. Web.

Hibberd, Dominic. "Wilfred Owen and the Georgians." The Review of English Studies ns 30.117 (1979): 28-40. Web.

Hipp, Daniel. ""By Degrees Regain[ing] Cool Peaceful Air in Wonder": Wilfred Owen's War Poetry as Psychological Therapy." The Journal of the Midwest Modern Language Association 35.1 (2002): 25-49. Web.

Johnson, George M. "'Purgatorial Passions': 'The Ghost' (a.k.a. Wilfred Owen) in Owen's Poetry." The Midwest Quarterly 51.2 (2010): 152+. Literature Resource Center. Web

Kerr, Douglas. "Brothers in Arms: Family Language in Wilfred Owen." The Review of English Studies 43.172 (1992): 518-34. Web.

Kerr, Douglas. "The Disciplines of the Wars: Army Training and the Language of Wilfred Owen." Modern Language Review 87.2 (Apr. 1992): 286-299. Rpt. in Poetry Criticism. Ed. Michelle Lee. Vol. 102. Detroit: Gale, 2010. Literature Resource Center. Web.

Lutes, Michael A. "Wilfred Owen: Overview." Gay & Lesbian Literature. Vol. 1. Detroit: Gale, 1994. Literature Resource Center. Web.

McClary, Ian. "Compassion and indignation in Owen and Sassoon: Ian McClary explores the tension between anger and pity in the war poetry of Wilfred Owen and Siegfried Sassoon." The English Review 15.3 (2005): 31+. Literature Resource Center. Web.

Musil, Caryn McTighe. "Wilfred Owen and Abram." Women's Studies 13.1 (1986): 49-61. Rpt. in Poetry Criticism. Ed. Carol T. Gaffke. Vol. 19. Detroit: Gale, 1997. Literature Resource Center. Web.

Musolino, Walter. "Physics and Metaphysics: Capture and Escape. Two War Poems of Wilfred Owen and Giuseppe Ungaretti." Forum Italicum 30.2 (Fall 1996): 311-319. Rpt. in Poetry Criticism. Ed. Lawrence J. Trudeau. Vol. 57. Detroit: Gale, 2004. Literature Resource Center. Web.

Najarian, James. ""Greater Love": Wilfred Owen, Keats, and a Tradition of Desire."Twentieth Century Literature 47.1 (2001): 20-38. Web.

Najmi, Samina. "The Whiteness of the Soldier-Speaker in Brian Turner's "Here, Bullet"" Rocky Mountain Review 65.1 (2011): 56-78. Web.

Norgate, Paul. "Wilfred Owen and the Soldier Poets." The Review of English Studies ns 40.160 (1989): 516-30. Web.

Pittock, Malcolm. "Wilfred Owen, Tailhade, Tolstoy, and Pacifism." The Review of English Studies 49.194 (1998): 154-66. Web.

Schweik, Susan. "Writing War Poetry like a Woman." Critical Inquiry 13.3 (1987): 532-56. Web.

Sen, Amartya. "Is Nationalism a Boon or a Curse?" Economic and Political Weekly 43.7 (2008): 39-44. Web.

Slawek, Tadeusz. ""Dark Pits of War": Wilfred Owen's Poetry and the Hermeneutics of War." Boundary 2 14.1/2 (1985): 309-31. Web.

Spanos, William V. "Culture and Colonization: The Imperial Imperatives of the Centered Circle." Boundary 2 23.1 (1996): 135-75. Web.

Spear, Hilda D. "Wilfred Owen and Poetic Truth." University of Kansas City Review 25.2 (Winter 1958): 110-116. Rpt. in Poetry Criticism. Ed. Carol T. Gaffke. Vol. 19. Detroit: Gale, 1997. Literature Resource Center. Web.

Stallworthy, Jon. "Wilfred Owen: Overview." Reference Guide to English Literature. Ed. D. L. Kirkpatrick. 2nd ed. Chicago: St. James Press, 1991. Literature Resource Center. Web.

Stephens, John, and Waterhouse Ruth. "Authorial Revision and Constraints on the Role of the Reader: Some Examples from Wilfred Owen." Poetics Today 8.1 (1987): 65-83. Web.

Sychterz, Jeffrey. "Scarred Narratives and Speaking Wounds: War Poetry and the Body." Pacific Coast Philology 44.2 (2009): 137-47. Web.

Tomlinson, Alan. "Strange Meeting in Strange Land: Wilfred Owen and Shelley." Studies in Romanticism 32.1 (Spring 1993): 75-95. Rpt. in Poetry Criticism. Ed. Michelle Lee. Vol. 102. Detroit: Gale, 2010. Literature Resource Center. Web.

Welland, D. S. R. "Half-Rhyme in Wilfred Owen: Its Derivation and Use." The Review of English Studies 1.3 (1950): 226-41. Web.

DISCARD